Narwhal

Unicorn of the Arctic

WRITTEN BY
CANDACE FLEMING

ILLUSTRATED BY
DEENA SO'OTEH

a·s·b
anne schwartz books

You are a narwhal—
shy,
swift,
small (for a whale).

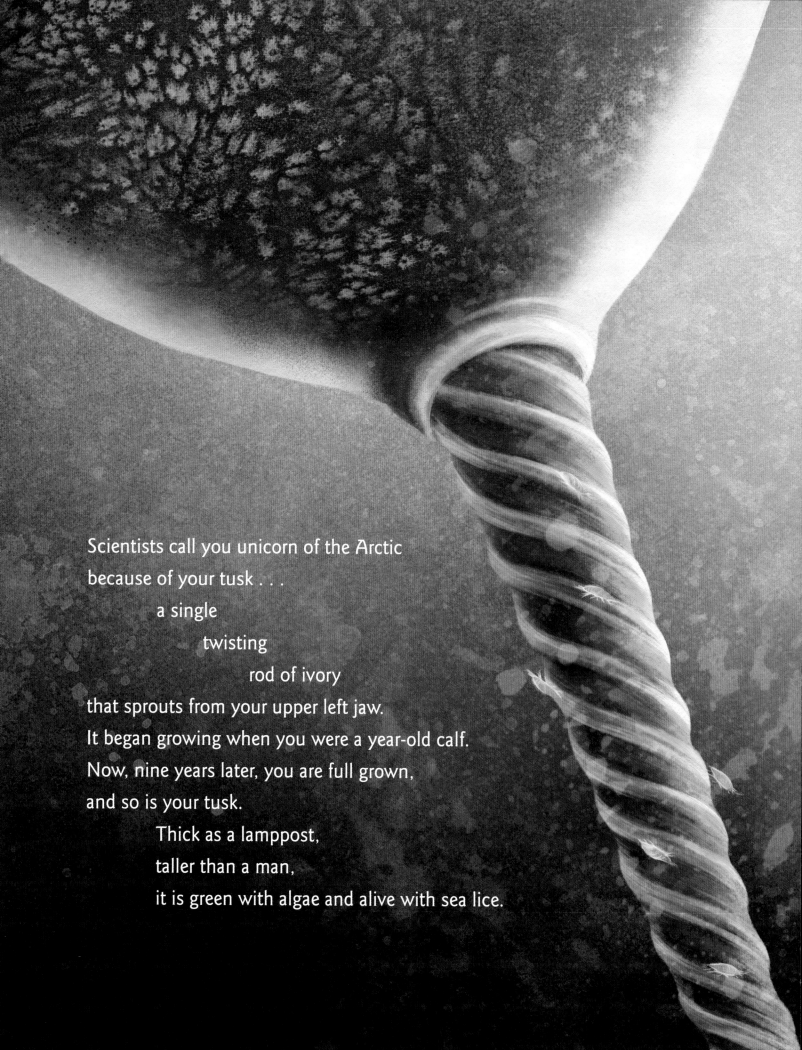

Scientists call you unicorn of the Arctic
because of your tusk . . .
            a single
                        twisting
                                    rod of ivory
that sprouts from your upper left jaw.
It began growing when you were a year-old calf.
Now, nine years later, you are full grown,
and so is your tusk.
            Thick as a lamppost,
            taller than a man,
            it is green with algae and alive with sea lice.

The other males in your pod have tusks, too.
But not the females
(except for a rare few).

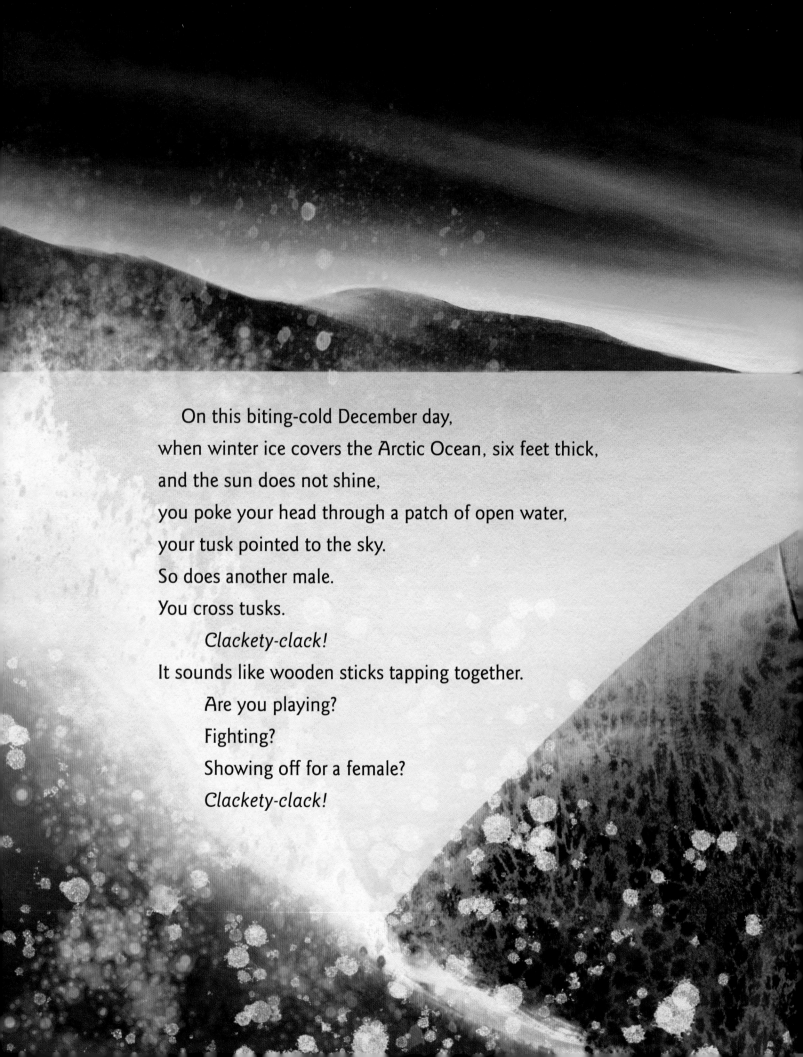

On this biting-cold December day,

when winter ice covers the Arctic Ocean, six feet thick,

and the sun does not shine,

you poke your head through a patch of open water,

your tusk pointed to the sky.

So does another male.

You cross tusks.

Clackety-clack!

It sounds like wooden sticks tapping together.

Are you playing?

Fighting?

Showing off for a female?

Clackety-clack!

As suddenly as it began, the joust ends.

You slip below the surface and swim beneath the ice.

You're not hurt.

Not this time.

But the scars on your head show you've been injured while tusking before.

The Arctic wind shrieks.

The strong sea currents shift.

And cracks of open water, called leads, appear in the ice.

You can't live without leads. How else would you breathe?

You surface in one.

Pshhht!

A fine mist of spray shoots from your blowhole. Then . . .

Ahhhh!

You draw in a lungful of sharp salt air.

Other narwhals come up to breathe, too, before curving back down.

Pshhht!

Ahhhh!

But a few remain on the surface to float, side by side by side.

You join them.

Overhead, the sky glows green.

Stars sparkle like ice chips.

You can make out snowy hummocks and towering ice ridges.

On the pack ice, a walrus lounges.

A bearded seal swims near.

Pshhht!

Ahhhh!

But hunger soon wakes you.
Time to dive!
Your tail pumps.
Your finless back arches.
Your cone-shaped body corkscrews
down . . .
down . . .
down . . .

All around you is the breathing of your podmates,
the whistle and wail of the wind,
the rasp and groan of the ever-shifting ice.

You sleep.

In minutes you are a mile deep and in total darkness.
Here you will need to use sound to see—echolocation

Tik-tik-tik-tik—
you listen to the echoes of your clicks
as they bounce off solid objects.
   Tik-tik-tik-tik—
a thousand clicks per second.
   Tik-tik-tik-tik—
there, Greenland halibut!

You flip upside down to feed,
      suck the fish into your toothless mouth,
         swallow it whole.
You stay down nearly half an hour,
      fishing and feeding,
until your lungs ache for air.
Flipping right side up, you shoot to the lead's surface.
      Pshhht!
         Ahhhh!

At the top of the world, winters are long. But by mid-June,
the twenty-four-hour darkness turns to twenty-four-hour sunlight.
The sea current warms.
The ice shifts.
The leads widen.

Time to migrate.

Your pod follows a route it has taken for generations,
    past looming bergs
    and narrow fjords
    and tall cliffs plated with ice.
Other pods join yours. With strong, graceful movements,
hundreds of you swim and dive in unison.

Along the way, calves are born.
Their mothers guide them,
    nudge them,
        nurse them underwater on fatty-rich milk.

By the end of July, your pod arrives at its summer grounds.
Here the water is shallower and warmer with just fragments of ice.
There is less food, too—fewer halibut, fewer cod, fewer squid.
Your stomach feels empty.
But you have put on extra blubber over the winter in preparation
for summer's lean meals. You will survive until winter, unless—

Five tall black fins like pirate sails slice through the bay's waters.
Orcas!

Prowling for dinner.
  Hunting for narwhals.
Your pod swims to the shallowest part of the bay.
You huddle together,
  calves in the middle,
  silent,
  still.
The predators swim closer.
They listen . . .

. . . for the shiver of a flipper,
            the tremble of a fluke.
But they do not find you.

The whales glide past.

By September, the days are short.

And ice has spread across the surface of your summer home.

Time to migrate back to your winter grounds,

     past tall cliffs plated in ice,

     narrow fjords,

     and looming bergs.

The lean summer has left you and the others hungry.

When you discover an inlet teeming with cod . . .

     how can you resist?

     You gorge.

Two days.

Three days.

On the fourth day, an early blizzard roars.

Ice covers the inlet and seals the narrow entrance shut.

You're trapped!

Frantically, your pod swims beneath the pane of ice,

      around and around,

      clicking and whistling.

There's no way out.

No place to breathe.

      Bam-bam-bam!

You bash your head against
the edges of a small crack.
You can't break through.
Bam-bam-bam!
Others bash, too.

At last, a patch of water opens.
A breathing hole.
 Pshhht!
  Ahhhh!

Within seconds, the hole churns with narwhals.
Your pod is packed in so tightly that you are lifted on
the backs of others each time you come up to breathe.
As you plunge down, you turn a somersault,
your tail waving in the air.
Water splashes. It freezes to the side of the hole.
So does the vapor from your pod's breath.

The hole grows smaller.
　　And smaller.
You move toward it, desperate to breathe.
Small bubbles rise to the surface with you.

You are discovered!

At that moment . . .
　　　Draaah-draaaaaah!
a podmate calls,
and you dive back down.
A way out of the inlet has been found!
As one, you follow a thread of open water.
　　　Pshhht!
　　　　Ahhhh!
　　　　　　Freedom!

By November, you are back in your winter home.
But you will return to the warmer shallows of the bay
        again and again,
        Along familiar routes,
        back and forth.
        Winter to summer.
        Summer to winter.
        For the next fifty seasons.

You are a narwhal—
        shy,
             swift,
                    small (for a whale),
the unicorn of the Arctic

Unicorn of the Arctic . . . Indeed!

We share our planet with roughly 170,000 narwhals. According to the International Union for Conservation of Nature (IUCN)—a global conservation organization that uses scientific criteria to evaluate extinction risks of animal species—narwhals are thriving. In 2017, the IUCN categorized them as an animal of "least concern."

Still, the narwhal's dependence on the ice-covered Arctic—an area drastically affected by climate change—means they could face problems in the future. Will narwhals be able to adapt to warmer water and shrinking ice? Will they be affected by human-made noise as the Arctic opens up to shipping, oil exploration, and tourism?

Researchers are working to answer these questions. Until recently, narwhals could only be observed during the summer months when they approached shore. The whales' behavior during the winter months remained largely a mystery. But advances in technology have begun to unravel it. Acoustic devices have given researchers an inkling of how narwhals communicate. DNA sequencing has helped to fill in the gaps in their evolutionary history. Heart monitors can gauge their levels of anxiety when encountering changes in their environment. And GPS tracking equipment that can withstand both bitter cold and the pressure of deep water has allowed researchers to follow their movements even in winter months.

Additionally, and just as importantly, scientists are partnering with Inuit and other indigenous communities to better understand the Arctic land, ice, and creatures. Over the centuries, Inuit culture has depended on the narwhal, and they have accumulated a deep knowledge of the animal, adapted and expanded from generation to generation. Inuit hunters know how to get close to the skittish whales without disturbing them. In the darkness, they can tell the difference between a beluga and a narwhal by the sound of its breathing. They can even search out a narwhal simply by its smell. Such information has been essential for the Inuit's survival in a dangerous, unpredictable region. And having Inuit as team members has been a boon to science, leading field investigations, formulating research questions, gathering and interpreting the data, and presenting the results. New questions are being asked, and new methods applied.

Here are just some of the amazing facts that observation and research have uncovered:

- The narwhal is an odontocete, or toothed whale. Curiously, though, the narwhal has no teeth. Instead, the male develops one long tooth, or tusk. Six to nine feet long, it sticks out of his upper jaw. Very rarely, a female grows a tusk, although it tends to be shorter than a male's and often falls off. Even more rarely, some males have been known to sprout *two* tusks.

- Researchers still aren't sure about the tusk's purpose. Some evidence suggests narwhals use their tusks like a club to stun their prey. Other studies indicate it might be a thermometer or a sensor to detect the amount of salt in the water. But most scientists think that tusks are meant to impress females. After all, they argue, if narwhals needed tusks to survive, females would have them, too. This theory would also explain why males cross tusks: they're showing off for the ladies. (Or maybe, say other scientists, the males are simply cleaning each other's teeth—a kind of social grooming.)

- Male narwhals can grow to be 16 feet long and weigh up to 4,000 pounds, while females reach 13 feet and 2,200 pounds. This might sound big, but narwhals are the smallest whales on the planet. Compare their size with the biggest: the Antarctic blue whale, at 98 feet long and 400,000 pounds.

- Narwhal calves—born during the summer migration—are a solid gray color. As they age, they develop the characteristic mottled black-and-white skin pattern. Most calves stay with their mothers for the first twenty months of their lives.

- Recent research, based on examination of narwhal eyeballs, suggests narwhals can live to be ninety years old.

- Narwhal pod sizes vary. Some can be as small as two or three; others consist of several hundred. Some are single-sexed, and others are mixed. During migration, these pods come together in the Arctic Ocean to form a huge group that travels together. In the winter, they again break into smaller pods to travel under the ice as it freezes.

- In the summer, narwhals dive to a depth between 98 and 980 feet, but spend about a third of their time near the surface. In the winter, when the sea's surface is 99 percent covered in sea ice, they can dive more than a mile down. An average winter dive is 2,625 feet and lasts around 25 minutes. Incredibly, they do this 18 to 25 times a day!

- Narwhals dive to depths where there is intense pressure. While humans can't go too deep before our rib cage collapses from the pressure, the narwhal has a collapsible rib cage. As the narwhal dives deeper, its rib cage shuts, enabling its lungs to deflate and its heart rate to decrease. This both protects its internal organs and minimizes its need for air. Additionally, the narwhal can close off blood flow to less essential organs and redirect it to more important body parts like the heart and brain.

- Orcas and polar bears are threats to narwhals, but the greatest danger may be the ice itself. Sassats, or entrapments, occur when sudden changes in temperature (such as an early fall snowstorm) freeze the open water shut. During an ice entrapment, hundreds of narwhals might be trapped under the ice with only a small breathing hole. Only the constant surfacing of the animals keeps them from being frozen underneath. This hole, with its access to fresh air, is a lifeline. But it is also a prison. Cut off from open water, trapped narwhals may die from starvation or suffocation, or become easy quarry for polar bears and human hunters.

- Narwhals use a system of clicks and whistles to detect fish, navigate in darkness, and communicate with their podmates. And while scientists have yet to decipher each sound's meaning, they know that the narwhal's language varies in summer and winter.

- Narwhals are predictable. For hundreds of thousands of years, they have participated in the annual cycle of migration, taking the same routes at exactly the same time each season, to winter and summer grounds that never vary.

Every day, we are learning more about the unicorn of the Arctic. Our job now is to put this knowledge to good use. We must make conservation policies that will protect narwhals. Sound decisions today will ensure we share our planet with these incredible creatures in the future.

To the incomparable Anne Schwartz
for thirty years of friendship . . . and eagle eyes. —C.F.

To my dearest mama and precious Yuna.
Thank you for your endless love and support.
It gave me wings. —D.S.O.

Acknowledgments

We are deeply indebted to Dr. Kristin Laidre, professor at the School of Aquatic and Fishery Sciences and senior principal researcher at the Polar Science Center, Applied Physics Lab, University of Washington, Seattle, not only for vetting the text and art of this book for accuracy, but also for her groundbreaking field-based studies on the ecology and population dynamics of Arctic marine mammals. This book sits on the shoulders of her vital and extraordinary research—it could not have been written without her vast knowledge of and deep commitment to polar ecology, marine conservation, and the impact of climate change.

Bibliography

Burdick, Alan. "The Strange, Fading Call of the Narwhal." newyorker.com/science/lab-notes/the-strange-fading-call-of-the-narwhal

Hall, Danielle. "Why a Tusk? The Real-life Unicorns of the Sea and the Tusks that Make Them Famous." ocean.si.edu/ocean-life/marine-mammals/why-tusk-real-life-unicorns-sea-and-tusks-make-them-famous

Katz, Brigit. "Narwhals Have Low Genetic Diversity—and They're Doing Fine." smithsonianmag.com/smart-news/narwhals-have-low-genetic-diversityand-theyre-doing-fine-180972111

Kennedy, Caitlyn. "A Narwhal's Tale: Surviving Sea Ice Change." climate.gov/news-features/features/narwhals-tale-surviving-sea-ice-change

Laidre, Kristin. "Narwhal FAQ." staff.washington.edu/klaidre/narwhal-faq

Laidre, Kristin L., and Mads Peter Heide-Jørgensen. 2005. "Arctic Sea Ice Trends and Narwhal Vulnerability." *Biological Conservation* 121 (4): 509–517.

Laidre, Kristin L., and Mads Peter Heide-Jørgensen. 2006. "Winter Feeding Intensity of Narwhals." *Marine Mammal Science* 21 (1): 45–57.

Laidre, Kristin L., and Mads Peter Heide-Jørgensen. 2011. "Life in the Lead: Extreme Densities of Narwhals *Monodon monoceros* in the Offshore Pack Ice." *Marine Ecology Progress Series* 423: 269–278.

McLeish, Todd. *Narwhals: Arctic Whales in a Melting World.* Seattle: University of Washington Press, 2013.

Sachs, Jessica Snyder. "Unlikely Partners in the Sea." nwf.org/Magazines/National-Wildlife/2009/Unlikely-Partners-In-The-Sea

Zimmer, Carl. "The Mystery of the Sea Unicorn." nationalgeographic.com/science/article/the-mystery-of-the-sea-unicorn